Alexander Graham Bell

Struan Reid

H **www.heinemann.co.uk**
Visit our website to find out more information about **Heinemann Library** books.

To order:
☎ Phone 44 (0) 1865 888066
📄 Send a fax to 44 (0) 1865 314091
💻 Visit the Heinemann Bookshop at www.heinemann.co.uk to browse our catalogue and order online.

First published in Great Britain by Heinemann Library,
Halley Court, Jordan Hill, Oxford OX2 8EJ,
a division of Reed Educational and Professional Publishing Ltd.
Heinemann is a registered trademark of Reed Educational and Professional Publishing Ltd.

OXFORD MELBOURNE AUCKLAND
JOHANNESBURG BLANTYRE GABORONE
IBADAN PORTSMOUTH (NH) USA CHICAGO

Designed by AMR
Illustrated by Art Construction
Originated by Ambassador Litho Ltd
Printed in Hong Kong/China

04 03 02 01 00
10 9 8 7 6 5 4 3 2 1

ISBN 0 431 10446 8

British Library Cataloguing in Publication Data
Reid, Struan
   Alexander Bell. – (Groundbreakers)
   1. Bell, Alexander Graham, 1847–1922 – Juvenile literature
   2. Inventors – Great Britain – Biography – Juvenile literature
   3. Scientists – Great Britain – Biography – Juvenile literature
   I. Title
   621.3'85'092

Acknowledgements
The Publishers would like to thank the following for permission to reproduce photographs:
Ann Ronan Picture Library: p. 36; Collections/Anthea Sieveking: p. 21; Hulton Deutsch Collection Limited: pp. 11, 16, 35, 37; Mansell/Katz Collection: pp. 31, 40; Mary Evans Picture Library: pp. 4, 7, 9, 12, 19, 26, 32, 38; Parks Canada, Alexander Graham Bell National Historic Site: pp. 8, 10, 15, 17, 18, 20, 24, 27, 29, 30, 33, 39, 41; Science Museum/Science and Society Picture Library: pp. 6, 13, 23, 25; Science Photo Library: pp. 5/Sheila Terry, 28, 42/Laguna Design, 43/Rosenfeld Images Ltd.

Cover photograph reproduced with permission of the Mansell/Katz Collection.

Every effort has been made to contact copyright holders of any material reproduced in this book. Any omissions will be rectified in subsequent printings if notice is given to the Publisher.

Any words appearing in the text in bold, **like this**, are explained in the glossary.

Contents

A changing world

Alexander Graham Bell in 1895, aged 48.

The life of Alexander Graham Bell spanned 75 years and covered an age of great invention, discovery and change. This period saw the height of the **Industrial Revolution** in Europe. Huge new factories powered by coal and steam were producing all sorts of goods. Some of the greatest changes took place in the field of communications. In 1847, the year in which Bell was born in Edinburgh, Scotland, railways and the electric **telegraph** were only just beginning to open up the world. By the time he died in 1922, people were flying in aeroplanes and the television was about to be invented.

A touch of brilliance

Early in his life, Bell was inspired by his deaf mother to teach **deaf-mutes** to speak. While he was investigating the methods of human speech and hearing, he also discovered the principles of the telephone. Several people contributed to the development of the telephone, but it was Bell's brilliant imagination that made it possible.

Bell's invention of the telephone revolutionized communications, and it continues to affect our lives today in ways that would have been unimaginable in his time. The telephone is one of the most important inventions of all time. Without it, many of the things we now take for granted – the radio, television, fax machines and the Internet – would not have been possible.

Many interests

The invention of the telephone in 1875 made Bell rich and famous while he was still only in his early thirties. But he did not stop there. The remaining 46 years of his life were packed with ideas and experiments. He invented a vacuum jacket, a forerunner of the **iron lung**, following the death of his own infant sons from breathing problems. He designed kites, aeroplanes and a hydrofoil boat. He helped to improve the breeding of sheep and co-founded the **National Geographic Society** of the USA. When Bell died, he was working on a project to distil drinking water from sea water. His interests and genius touched many areas, but Bell's name is known all over the world mainly for his invention of the telephone.

An early Bell telephone in use. In Bell's original telephone system the speaker and the receiver were identical.

Early life

Alexander Bell was born in Edinburgh, Scotland, on 3 March 1847. He was always known in his family as Aleck. He was the second son of Alexander Melville Bell, Professor of **Elocution** and the Art of Speech at Edinburgh University. Professor Bell helped people with problems such as stammering to talk clearly.

Growing up in Edinburgh

Professor Bell's three sons, Melville, Aleck and Edward, were at first taught at home by their mother, Eliza Bell. She taught the three boys the usual school subjects, such as history and mathematics, but she also gave them drawing and music lessons. Aleck was an excellent pianist, and music played a very important part in his childhood. Eliza had been deaf since childhood and the boys learned to communicate with her by using sign language. This was to have a profound influence on the interests and later career of young Aleck.

*Eliza Grace Bell, Aleck's mother. Eliza Bell had been deaf from birth. Aleck was to spend much of his adult life developing and teaching deaf and **deaf-mute** people to communicate.*

ELIZA GRACE SYMONDS

Eliza Grace Symonds (1810–97) was an Englishwoman. She had three younger brothers. Her father was a surgeon in the Royal Navy and died in 1818 when Eliza was 9 years old. Although she had been deaf from childhood, she was very intelligent and widely read. She was 10 years older than Alexander Melville Bell, and when they first met she was working as a teacher of drawing and as a painter of miniatures. They were married on 19 July 1844.

Edinburgh, like most large cities of the time, was smoky and dirty, and Aleck's father was concerned for his family's health. He bought a second house outside Edinburgh near the sea, so that the family could get out of the city and enjoy the fresh air. Aleck loved the time the family spent there and enjoyed going for walks along the beaches, studying the plants, birds and animals. He also spent a lot of his time trying to invent things.

In 1858, at the age of 11, Aleck was sent away to study at the Royal Edinburgh High School. But his time there was not a success as he disliked the strict discipline at the school. He chose to study Latin and Greek but had no particular interest in the formal lessons. After four years at the school, he left without any proper qualifications.

A new name

When Aleck was 11 years old, a former pupil of his father's called Alexander Graham visited the family. Aleck liked the man's name and, as a show of independence from his father and because his brothers had two first names, he added the name Graham to his own. From then on he was to be called Alexander Graham Bell.

Edinburgh University, where Aleck's father, Alexander Melville Bell, was Professor of Elocution and the Art of Speech.

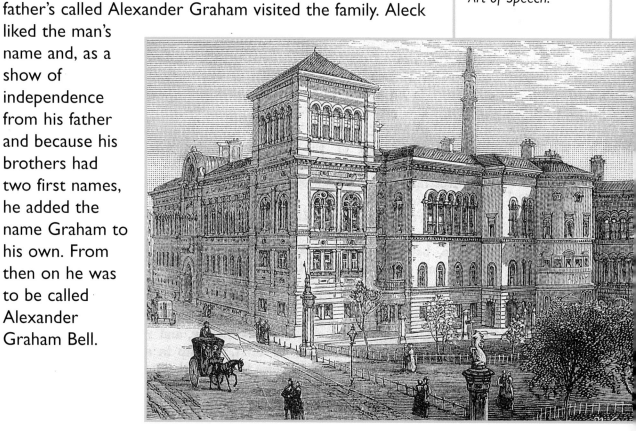

7

A year in London

Aleck's father was worried about his son's poor performance at school and wrote to his own father in London. The old man believed that his grandson needed the space to develop his own personality away from the domineering characters of his father and brothers. He suggested that Aleck should come and stay with him in London. Aleck's father agreed, and in October 1862 Aleck, aged 15, boarded the train south. He wrote later that this was 'the turning point of my whole career'.

Aleck's grandfather, Alexander Bell, was the first member of the Bell family to become interested in studying and teaching speech.

ALEXANDER BELL

Aleck's grandfather, another Alexander Bell (1790–1865), had begun his working life as a shoemaker in Scotland. He later became an actor and teacher of **elocution** at the University of St Andrews in Scotland. It was during this period that he became interested in speech difficulties, especially stammering. He moved south to London where he opened a school of speech. His son (Aleck's father), and later Aleck himself, continued with this family profession.

An inspiring teacher

Aleck's grandfather was strict and insisted that his grandson dressed neatly every day and studied hard. Together they read through the plays of Shakespeare and Aleck learned many of the speeches by heart. Aleck's grandfather was also a speech expert, and taught Aleck his special skills. Although he was strict, he inspired Aleck in a way that his father and teachers had been unable to do. Aleck respected his grandfather and they got on well with each other.

The London that Aleck visited was a thriving industrial city. The River Thames was a busy commercial waterway, and the London skyline was dominated by church spires and brick chimneys.

In the early summer of 1863, Aleck's father travelled south to London, and was amazed to see how different his son was. Aleck had grown tall and broad. He had changed from a clumsy, untidy schoolboy into a well-dressed and self-confident young man.

Another reason for Alexander Melville's trip to London was to meet an inventor called Charles Wheatstone. Wheatstone had invented the first effective electric **telegraph** and, in the 1820s, he had also produced a crude speaking machine. He gave Aleck and his father a demonstration of this old machine and lent them detailed diagrams.

PUBLIC SPEAKING

As Aleck was growing up, lessons in elocution were very popular. Public lectures were being given in many cities on the new scientific discoveries, inventions and the exploration of the world. There were no microphones or loud-speakers in those days, so it was important that the lecturers were able to speak clearly, without shouting.

Aleck at the age of 16 or 17.

'I think you should implicitly surrender yourself to Papa's judgement in this matter.'

(Aleck's mother Eliza writing to him to try and settle an argument between him and his father about Aleck's work)

After his year in London, Aleck returned to Edinburgh with his father. There, he and his brother Melville studied Wheatstone's designs for the talking machine, and built an improved version. They used a tin tube, a wooden box, cotton and rubber. By blowing through the tube they could make it say, 'Mama'. This project taught Aleck much about how the human voice worked.

Breaking free

However, soon after Aleck was back with his family, his father once again treated him like a small boy. He felt stifled by his parents, and became restless and depressed. He wanted to break free and even considered running away to sea. At the last minute he changed his mind and decided instead to become a teacher. He applied for a job as a student-teacher at a boarding school called Weston House in Elgin, north of Edinburgh.

Aleck's father now realized that it was time for his two older sons to start a new life. Melville went to study at Edinburgh University and, in August 1863, Aleck took up his position of teacher of music and **elocution** at Weston House. He was just 16 years old. Even though some of the students were older than their new teacher, the self-confidence Aleck had acquired in London made him seem very responsible and much older than he really was.

At this time, Aleck was also studying the experiments on **acoustics** (sound) of a German scientist called Hermann von Helmholtz. Helmholtz had managed to produce artificial vowel sounds with a machine, using tuning forks and electricity. Aleck believed that Helmholtz had actually sent the sounds by electricity through a wire, in the same way **telegraph** messages were sent, rather than just making the sounds himself. Although Aleck was mistaken in this idea, it led him to think about the possibility of sending speech over distances along an electric wire.

Hermann von Helmholtz (1821–94). Aleck studied Helmholtz's experiments on acoustics. These studies led him to consider whether it might be possible to send speech along electric wires.

Aleck taught for a year at the school and then spent a year at Edinburgh University, where he studied Latin and Greek. He returned to Weston House in September 1865 and, now aged 18, was promoted to assistant master. He then spent a year teaching at Somerset College in Bath, England.

All the while, Aleck continued his studies of **phonetics** (human speech). He would spend hours in his room experimenting with his voice, touching his throat and cheeks with his fingers while making different vowel sounds and feeling the vibrations. The results of his experiments sometimes conflicted with his father's ideas, but Aleck was beginning to make great advances of his own in the field of phonetics.

Discoveries before Bell

Michael Faraday was a brilliant scientist and an excellent speaker, who communicated his ideas to the public through his lectures.

Much of the background work and the technology that made the telephone possible had been in existence for many years before Aleck was even born. But with imagination and hard work he gathered together the pieces of information and organized them in such a way as to come up with the design for the first telephone.

Electricity and magnetism

An English scientist called Michael Faraday (1791–1867) had become very interested in the relationship between electricity and **magnetism**. People had known about magnetism for thousands of years, and many people believed that electricity and magnetism must be related in some way. In 1820, a Danish scientist called Hans Oersted (1777–1851) noticed that a wire with an electric current running through it acted like a magnet, making the needle move on a compass lying nearby.

Faraday then found that when he charged a coil of wire with electricity, an electric current also flowed in another, separate wire coil nearby. He believed that this second current must be generated by the magnetic effect of the first one.

In 1823, the English scientist William Sturgeon (1783–1850) made the first **electromagnet**. By passing an electric current through a wire wrapped round an iron bar, he created a magnet which could lift 20 times its own weight.

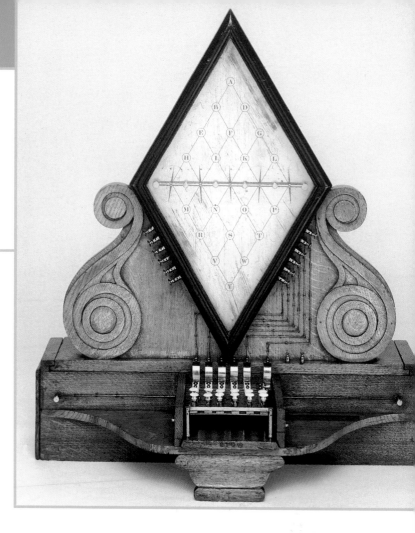

Messages along wires

The first effective electric **telegraph** was produced in 1837 by two English inventors called William Cooke (1806–79) and Charles Wheatstone (1802–75). The telegraph worked on the principle of **electromagnetism**. It had five needles connected to wires. When an electric current flowed through the wires, the needles pointed to letters on a grid, spelling out the message. The first commercial telegraph line was opened in London in 1839, connecting Paddington Station and West Drayton, 21 kilometres (13 miles) away. The first telegraph line in Edinburgh was opened in 1847, the year of Aleck's birth.

In 1843, an American artist called Samuel Morse (1791–1872) designed a new telegraph code which replaced the one used by Cooke and Wheatstone. This Morse code, as it is known, uses signals transmitted electrically, consisting of short dots and long dashes to indicate letters.

In 1858, Charles Wheatstone devised an automatic telegraph system. Operators punched a message in Morse code on to a paper tape which ran through a transmitter. A pen at the other end drew the signal on to another paper tape. Eventually, the pen was replaced with a 'sounder', which converted the dots and dashes into long and short sounds. This coded message was written down and then translated by the operator.

Return to London

In April 1865 Aleck's grandfather died and his son, Alexander Melville Bell, decided that the family work in **elocution** and **phonetics** should be continued in London. He, his wife and their youngest son Edward travelled south and moved into Alexander Bell's old house.

Visible Speech

For many years Aleck's father had been trying to devise a special alphabet to help people with speech difficulties, in which the signs would stand for sounds rather than letters. In this way any noise in any language could be written down and read by someone else. After fifteen years of hard work, he finally produced his alphabet, which he called 'Visible Speech'. In the Visible Speech system each set of symbols showed the positions of the mouth, tongue, lips and throat used to make a particular sound. In this way, the sounds themselves could be written down.

Some numbers and words using the Visible Speech alphabet. There were 34 symbols in the Visible Speech alphabet. Each one stands for a sound rather than a letter.

1 ƎIƱ

2 ƱƖƖ

3 ƁƜƱƖƖ

4 ƎƖƳ

5 ƎƖƳƎ

6 ƘIƆƘ

7 ƘIƎƱƖ

8 ƈƮƱ

Ǝ꜀Ɑ

ƘƆƖ

OƖꜪƱꟿƱ

ƱƆƎ

ƎƖƆƁƱ

Aleck's two brothers and his parents. His younger brother Edward, who died of tuberculosis in 1867, is on the right.

While Aleck was still teaching in Bath, tragedy struck the Bell family. Both Aleck's brothers had suffered from ill health through much of their lives. In 1867 his younger brother Edward died of the lung disease tuberculosis. The family was devastated and Aleck hurried from Bath to London to be with them.

In 1868 Aleck enrolled as a student at London University to study **anatomy** and **physiology**. He threw himself into his studies and also helped his father to teach Visible Speech. At the same time he started a project of his own, teaching deaf children the basics of speech.

In Bell's words:

'Edward died this morning at ten minutes to four o'clock. He was only 18 years and 8 months old.'

(From Aleck's diary of 1867)

That same year Aleck's father went on a lecture tour around North America to demonstrate Visible Speech. No one in Britain had been very interested in the method, and he thought that it might receive more attention in North America. The trip was a great success, and Aleck's father began to think that the family's future might lie in North America.

He returned to London brimming with the success of his American tour. Then tragedy struck the family a second time. In 1870 Aleck's remaining brother Melville suddenly fell ill and died. The family, just recovering from their first loss, was shattered once again. Aleck's father decided that it was now time to leave for a new life in North America.

A new life in North America

Families boarding a ship bound for Canada in 1870. Like the Bells, they plan to start new lives in North America.

At first Aleck wanted to stay in England. His studies at London University were going well. He also had a girlfriend called Marie Eccleston, and they were thinking of getting married. Aleck was at a crossroads in his life and he had to decide which way to go.

An important decision

Aleck was now his parents' last surviving child, and he finally decided that it was his responsibility to accompany them to their new life in North America. With sad farewells, the small family group set sail on 21 July 1870, from the port of Liverpool, for Quebec in Canada. Aleck was 23 years old and a brand new chapter in his life was now beginning.

The Bells arrived in Quebec on 1 August 1870. By the end of their first week in Canada, Aleck's father had bought a handsome white-painted house at Tutela Heights, in Ontario. It stood in 4 hectares of land, and had an orchard with apple, plum, pear and peach trees. The Bells moved in just in time to harvest the fruit!

The Bells' new house was not far from the Niagara Falls and the air was clean and fresh. Aleck spent the remaining weeks of the summer relaxing, lying among the trees, and reading and writing. It reminded him of his family holidays in the countryside outside Edinburgh. His health had also suffered from the smoky London atmosphere, but by the autumn he was feeling fit and rested and was ready to begin working.

Starting again

Aleck's father, meanwhile, was busy re-establishing contacts he had made on his lecture tour of America. He visited a number of cities, where he gave lectures on his Visible Speech system. While in Boston, he met Sarah Fuller, who ran a school for deaf children. She was very interested in Visible Speech and wanted it taught at her school. Aleck's father wrote home and mentioned this. Aleck immediately wrote back to his father to say that he would be very happy to teach at the school, even if he was not paid for it.

Aleck's father agreed, and Aleck was offered an appointment for one month at the Boston School for **Deaf-Mutes** (later the Horace Mann School). He was to start work the next spring.

> **In Bell's words:**
>
> *'I shall not personally object to teaching Visible Speech in some well-known institution if you would get an appointment – even if it was not remunerative.'*
>
> (Letter from Aleck to his father in 1870)

The Bells' house at Tutela Heights, Ontario, Canada.

17

The successful teacher

On 5 April 1871, a fine spring day, Aleck stepped out of the train in Boston and went to his new lodgings. He was met by his landlady, who greeted him warmly. The next day he was given a tour of the city. Of all the buildings there, Aleck was particularly impressed by the large public library on Boylston Street and by the Boston Institute of Technology.

Sarah Fuller

Sarah Fuller (1836–1927) was a brilliant teacher of deaf children. She was born on a farm in Weston, Massachusetts, USA, and started teaching in 1855. Her career teaching deaf children began when she met the Reverend Dexter King, one of the founders of the Clarke School for the Deaf in Northampton, Massachusetts. Sarah Fuller was appointed principal of the school.

In 1869 the Boston School for **Deaf-Mutes** (later renamed the Horace Mann School for the Deaf) was founded. This was the first public day school for the deaf in the USA. Sarah Fuller was appointed its first principal and she worked there until 1910. The school was the first to adopt Visible Speech as an aid to teaching. She and Aleck kept in touch throughout their lives.

> **In Bell's words:**
>
> *'I never saw Love, Goodness and Firmness so blended in one face before.'*
>
> (Aleck's description of Sarah Fuller after he had just met her)

The Boston School for Deaf-Mutes, 1871. Alexander Bell is in the top row on the right. Sarah Fuller is in the fourth row, second from the left.

Great impressions

Aleck made an immediate impact with Visible Speech at Miss Fuller's school. By the end of the first day, even the youngest students had made great progress.

Aleck worked extremely hard over the following months at a number of schools. All the time he had to improve and adjust his teaching methods. But his skills were now so much in demand that he had to turn down offers of work in other parts of the country.

Late 19th-century Boston was an attractive and prosperous city.

Recipe for success

As the end of term exams approached, Aleck became very nervous about the results. His work was still based on trial and error, and he was not sure whether his teaching methods had really been successful. But he need not have worried. The superintendent of the Boston schools declared that the results were 'more than satisfactory, they are wonderful!' He went on to say that Aleck's teaching methods 'must speedily revolutionize the teaching in all … deaf-mute schools'. The Visible Speech system eventually became the standard method in North America for teaching the deaf to talk.

Aleck spent the summer holidays with his parents in their home in Ontario. After a rewarding but exhausting time in Boston, he relaxed by going for long walks, riding and swimming. Tutela Heights was a haven that enabled him to rest completely. It also allowed him the time to think, and while he was there he started to put together a long-term plan to open his own school for teaching deaf people.

Private pupils

Mabel Hubbard became deaf at the age of 5, as a result of scarlet fever. In 1872 Aleck took her on as a private pupil. Little did he know that she would turn out to be a special person in his life.

THERESA DUDLEY

One of Aleck's students was a girl of 17 called Theresa Dudley. Up until then, Aleck had been teaching students whose deafness had been caused by illness or accident. But Theresa had been deaf from birth and so had never heard a sound. Aleck kept a detailed diary of his work with her, which recorded how, very slowly, he managed to get Theresa first to understand speech and eventually to speak herself.

While he was on vacation in Ontario, Aleck had placed an advertisement in the newspapers offering his services as a private tutor. But when he returned to Boston in September, he found that he had received only four responses. He began teaching this small group of students in his lodgings. He was now 24 years old.

Patient guidance

Aleck would demonstrate to his students how the sounds of human speech are produced by the very fast vibrations of the vocal cords in the voice box. He showed how the speed and sound of these vibrations could be changed by changing the position of the mouth, teeth and tongue.

Aleck encouraged his students to touch his neck, jaw, cheeks, mouth and lips. When he spoke they could feel the vibrations. Then they would feel their own necks and mouths and try to make sounds that produced the same vibrations they had felt in him.

In Bell's words:

'I cannot describe to you the effect produced ... I believe this experiment constitutes an epoch in the history of the education of the deaf and dumb.'

(Letter from Aleck to his parents reporting his work with Theresa Dudley)

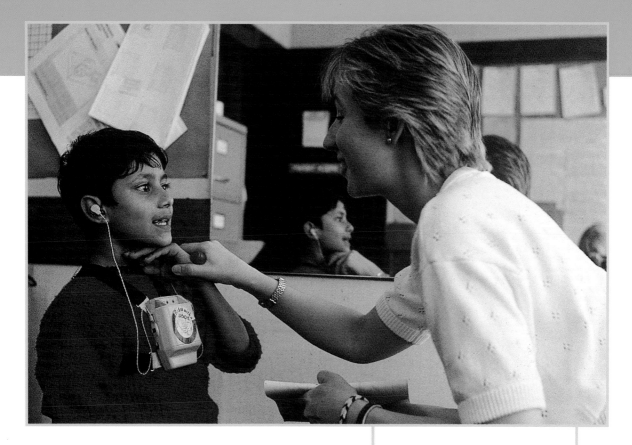

Aleck tried to teach using patience and encouragement. This was quite different from the method of strictness and punishment that was normally used at that time. In this way he built up confidence and helped children who were expected never to speak. He brought them great happiness and himself great satisfaction.

Aleck continued to teach his small group of students. In March 1872, he began teaching at the Clarke School for the Deaf in Northampton, Massachusetts and at a school in Hartford, Connecticut. His teaching methods were once again a great success. Classes were very big.

At the end of September 1872, Aleck returned to Boston and rented two rooms at Number 35 West Newton Street. This was to be the first permanent home of his own in the United States. There he gave lessons to twelve private pupils.

Deaf children today are still taught to speak by feeling the vibrations that speech creates in their vocal chords.

'With these simple motions ... he has the whole two hundred and fifty voices, from deep bass to shrill treble, under sufficient control to make them roar in concert or die away softly ... The pupils like it.'

(From an account of one of Aleck's lessons at the Clarke School)

Improving the telegraph

Aleck had never forgotten the studies he made back in London and Edinburgh on Helmholtz's experiments on **acoustics**. During his time as a teacher, he spent many evenings in his rooms trying to improve the design of the electric **telegraph**.

More than one message

A problem with the telegraph was that it could send only one message at a time in each direction. This meant that lines were always busy and people had to queue to send messages. Aleck's plan was to design a machine that could 'read' several messages transmitted at the same time along one wire. This would increase the number of messages the telegraph could handle, so making it much quicker and cheaper to send them. He called his machine a 'harmonic telegraph'.

The harmonic telegraph

Aleck's idea for a harmonic telegraph came from his knowledge of music and sound. If two string instruments, such as pianos or guitars, are placed next to each other and a note is played on one, the same note can be heard in the same string on the other instrument. This is called *resonance*, and the sound is carried from one instrument to the other by vibrations in the air.

When two musical instruments, such as pianos or guitars, are placed near each other and one of the strings on one of the instruments is hit or plucked, the corresponding string in the other instrument will begin to vibrate 'in sympathy'. This is caused by sound waves passing from one to the other and it is known as resonance.

Aleck believed he could apply this principle of resonance to the telegraph by using vibrating electricity instead of air. He used a series of vibrating strips of metal attached to a wire to make an electric current switch on and off at the same rate as the vibrations in the metal strips.

At the other end of the wire, **electromagnets** were switched on and off by the electric current. Next to each electromagnet was another metal strip which would be attracted by the electromagnet and vibrate in resonance with the matching strip at the other end. In this way, each metal strip and its pair at the other end could send and receive its own messages without interfering with others being sent on the same wire.

Exhausting work

Aleck's experimental work in the evenings was exhausting. His idea for the harmonic telegraph may have been a simple one, but he was not sure about the electrical side of it, and it took him a whole year to make it work.

After a year of teaching by day and then experimenting by night, Aleck was worn out. He returned to his parents' house for the Christmas vacation of 1872. Rest and relaxation restored his health.

In Aleck's mother's words:

'We are grieved but not surprised at your being unwell. You undertake too much ... We will talk of your invention ... when you are home ... I want you not to think about it just now.'

On the road to success

In September 1873, at the age of just 26, Aleck was appointed Professor of Vocal **Physiology** at the new Boston University. Boston University had opened in 1869, and was the first American university to admit women students.

Growing interest

As well as teaching at the university, Aleck continued his work with his private pupils. This put him in touch with some very important figures in Boston society who would have a great influence on his career. One of his pupils was Georgie Sanders, the 6-year-old son of a rich Boston businessman called Thomas Sanders. Another pupil was Mabel Hubbard, the 15-year-old daughter of the influential lawyer Gardiner Hubbard.

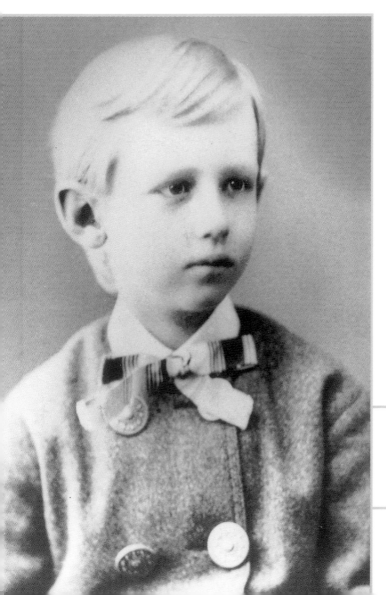

Meanwhile, whenever he had any free time, Aleck continued with his experiments on the **telegraph**. He was eager for fame and fortune, and he knew that if he managed to design a multiple telegraph that could transmit a number of messages at the same time he would become very rich. But his experiments were hindered by his lack of electrical knowledge.

Aleck often went to an electrical shop in Boston owned by a man called Charles Williams to buy pieces of equipment for his experiments.

Georgie Sanders had been born deaf. After a year of lessons with Aleck, he was able to read and spell.

One of the assistants working in Williams' shop was a young man called Thomas Watson. Watson was a brilliant electrician, and soon he was helping Aleck with his experiments.

Thomas Sanders and Gardiner Hubbard were very interested in Aleck's experiments with the telegraph, and they agreed to become his financial backers. With their help, Aleck was now able to afford to pay for an assistant. He chose Thomas Watson for the job.

Aleck needed all the assistance he could get, because there were other inventors also working hard on improving the telegraph. One of these was Elisha Gray of Chicago, and Aleck wrote that it was 'a neck-and-neck race between Mr. Gray and myself who shall complete an apparatus first'. Aleck and Gray had heard of each other's work through mutual contacts. The heat was on – and only time would tell who would reach the goal first.

Thomas Watson, the brilliant electrical engineer who worked with Aleck to develop the telephone.

THOMAS WATSON

Thomas Watson (1854–1934) was born in Salem, Massachusetts, the son of a stable foreman. He joined Charles Williams' shop when he was 18 years old, and within two years he was one of the best workmen in the shop. He worked with Aleck for more than five years, and would be one of the founders of the Bell Telephone Company. He later took up farming and eventually became a successful shipbuilder.

A change of direction

The race to design an improved **telegraph** was fierce, and Bell and Watson worked hard over the following months. Sometimes Aleck worked through the night until dawn. Finally, on 25 February 1875, Aleck **patented** a device he called an 'autograph telegraph' (writing telegraph). This used the multiple telegraph system to make dots and dashes on a strip of paper. This was a primitive version of the modern facsimile (fax) machine.

The famous physicist Joseph Henry, whose encouragement gave Aleck the confidence to pursue his work on the telephone.

In March that year, Aleck travelled to Washington to meet the famous scientist Joseph Henry, director of the **Smithsonian Institution**. Bell gave him a demonstration of all he had achieved so far in his telegraph experiments. He also asked Henry for his opinion on an idea he had for transmitting the human voice by using a telegraph with a **diaphragm** instead of metal strips. Henry was very interested and replied that Aleck had 'the germ of a great invention'. But when Aleck said that he did not have the electrical knowledge needed to continue with this work, Henry told him, 'Get it!'

In Bell's words:

'I cannot tell you how much these two words have encouraged me.'

(Aleck writing to his parents, soon after his meeting with Joseph Henry)

Joseph Henry (1797–1878) was one of America's most famous scientists. He was born of Scottish parents and became professor of **Natural Philosophy** at Princeton University in 1832, and the first director of the Smithsonian Institution in 1846. As a young man he had experimented with **electromagnetism** and designed the first electric telegraph. His encouragement was crucial and played a vital part in Aleck's eventual success.

Gardiner Hubbard, whose financial backing made it possible for Aleck to work first on improving the telegraph, and then on developing the telephone.

Henry's encouragement gave Aleck the confidence he needed to develop his idea of the telephone. He decided to drop out of the telegraph race and to concentrate only on the telephone. But in order to devote as much time as possible to this new work, Aleck sent away all his pupils, except Georgie Sanders and Mabel Hubbard. This meant that he now had very little money to live on, and he was soon forced to borrow from Thomas Watson.

Gardiner Hubbard was keen that Aleck should continue with his work on the telegraph, as he felt that it would be there that their fortune would be made. But Aleck was growing more and more certain that he was on the verge of a breakthrough in the development of the telephone. Unknown to him, it would be only a matter of weeks before that happened.

In Bell's words:

'I think that the transmission of the human voice is much more nearly at hand than I had supposed.'

(From a letter to Aleck's parents)

A happy accident

On 2 June 1875, an extremely hot day in Boston, Aleck and Thomas Watson were working in the attic rooms of Charles Williams' shop and making adjustments to the multiple **telegraph**. They were in two separate rooms, Aleck with three transmitters and three receivers in one room, connected by a wire to three receivers in the next-door room, where Watson was sitting. Batteries supplied electricity to the system. They were struggling to improve the design and Aleck was getting hot and impatient.

Falling into place

When he pressed the keys of the first two transmitters, the receivers in both rooms responded correctly. But when he tried the third transmitter, the metal strip on Watson's receiver did not respond. Aleck thought that the strip must have become stuck and switched off the transmitters and batteries. As Watson plucked the strip to work it free, it vibrated up and down. Aleck noticed that the corresponding receiving strip also started to vibrate, even though the electric current had been switched off.

Bursting with excitement, he ran next door and told Watson to continue plucking the metal strip and then ran back to his own room. To his delight, the strip continued to vibrate. As Watson continued plucking his strip, the metal strip on Aleck's receiver not only continued to vibrate but also made a sound.

Reconstruction of Bell and Watson's laboratory in Williams' shop, Boston.

Aleck suddenly realized what was happening. As Watson's metal strip vibrated up and down when he plucked it, it produced an electric current in the wire all by itself. This is the principle known as *electromagnetic induction* and is the basis of the telephone. As the strip vibrated, the electric current in the wire changed in strength, which made the receiver strip at Aleck's end vibrate in the same way. In that moment, on that hot evening at the beginning of June 1875, the telephone was born.

Electromagnetic induction

If a magnet or piece of magnetized metal is placed near a wire, an electric current will be 'induced' (generated) in the wire. The **magnetic field** must move or vary in strength in relation to the wire in order for the electricity to flow continuously.

Two years before his accidental discovery, in 1873, Aleck had come up with the idea of using a thin, magnetized metal strip vibrating at a set speed next to a wire. He thought that an electric current would be induced in the wire at the same speed of vibration. But he also thought it would be of no practical use as the electricity would be too weak. But this turned out to be the basis of the telephone.

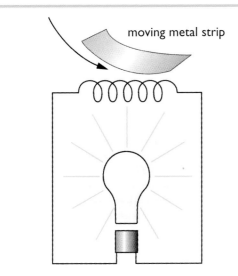

moving metal strip

This diagram shows the principle of electromagnetic induction.

When the strip is close to the wire, the electric current is strong so the light bulb is brighter.

When the strip moves away from the wire, the light bulb dims.

A growing love

Over the following days, Aleck and Watson worked on perfecting the instrument. Aleck felt that for the transmission of speech, a **diaphragm** would be better than a series of metal strips. He drew a rough design which he gave to Watson, who built a new machine in time for testing the next evening.

Trial and error

The device consisted of a wooden frame holding a sound receiver with a metal strip touching a diaphragm made of **parchment**. But when they tested it, the diaphragm was too tight and thin and it broke. So they tried a thicker, stronger diaphragm which, although it transmitted sounds when they spoke into it, did not allow them to make out any words. A lot more work needed to be done.

Mabel Hubbard as a young woman.

Aleck was discouraged by these failures, and work on the telephone stopped for eight months when Watson fell ill, even though they were on the verge of a breakthrough. A number of other things were also developing which now occupied Aleck's mind.

New concerns

Since March 1875, Aleck had been visiting the Hubbard home a few times each week to keep Gardiner Hubbard informed of the experimental work on the multiple **telegraph**, and also to continue his daughter Mabel's speech lessons. She was now 17 years old and Aleck was 28. This was quite an age difference, but Aleck realized that he was beginning to fall in love with his young pupil.

Aleck had fallen out of favour with Gardiner Hubbard, as he had abandoned work on the telegraph in favour of the telephone. Because of this, Hubbard was opposed to Aleck's interest in his daughter at first. But, after some gentle persuasion, Mrs Hubbard and Mabel eventually won him round, and on 25 November 1875, Thanksgiving Day and Mabel's 18th birthday, she and Aleck became engaged.

Aleck Bell in 1876, the year after his engagement to Mabel Hubbard.

In Bell's words:

'I have discovered that my interest in my dear pupil ... has ripened into a far deeper feeling ... I have learned to love her.'

(Part of a letter from Aleck to Mabel's mother)

Who was first?

Aleck's life was about to change in all kinds of ways. In January 1876 he moved into rented rooms at the top of a house in Exeter Place, Boston. He turned one of his two rooms into a workshop. This was a critical time in his work on the telephone. He was still teaching during the day, and during the night continued his work on the telephone. However, he had to apply for a **patent** for his telephone before anyone got there first.

Unseen complications

Aleck completed a detailed patent application in January 1876. As he was still a British citizen, he wanted to submit his telephone patent in Britain first. It was all arranged, but the person he had entrusted to make the application in Britain decided at the last moment not to submit it as he felt that the telephone had no future.

At this point Mabel's father stepped in. Frustrated by all the delay, he acted on Aleck's behalf and made a formal application for the telephone patent in Washington on 14 February 1876. He was only just in time, because a few hours later a lawyer acting for Elisha Gray submitted a document claiming that he (Gray) had invented a device for 'transmitting conversations through an electric circuit'. The document would prevent others from trying to make a telephone.

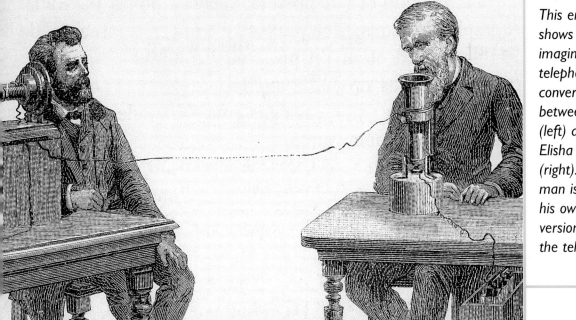

This engraving shows an imaginary telephone conversation between Aleck (left) and Elisha Gray (right). Each man is using his own version of the telephone.

As Gray had never tried out his device, he had no proof that it worked. Aleck was eventually awarded the patent for the telephone on 7 March 1876, four days after his 29th birthday. It was to become one of the most valuable patents in history.

Elisha Gray conceded defeat, but later both he and other inventors contested Aleck's patent. We now know that Gray's design would, in fact, have worked much better than Aleck's. It was only a sketch, however – he had never built his device so it had never been tested. Hundreds of **lawsuits** were brought against Aleck over the following years, but they all failed. In the race to make a telephone, Aleck had passed the winning-post first.

Bell's original patent – US Patent number 174,465 – for the telephone, dated 7 March 1876.

The power of patents

A patent is a detailed description of an invention. This description is registered and held by the patent office to record the 'first and true inventor'. The person issued with the patent is known as the *patentee*. For a set number of years, the patentee is granted the exclusive right to make, use or sell the invention. The patentee can also grant this right to someone else or they can sell the patent to someone else. If an invention becomes successful, as the telephone did, a patent is extremely valuable because the person who has the patent for an invention also earns the money from the invention.

The first telephone

On the day he was awarded the **patent** for the telephone, Aleck returned to Boston. Although he had won the race against Elisha Gray, there was still a lot more work to do on improving the telephone design. He made a drawing of another design and once again gave it to Thomas Watson to make.

Improved design

The new telephone equipment contained a **diaphragm** which vibrated when spoken into. A wire was attached to the diaphragm and vibrated with it. This vibration made the wire dip into a dish filled with a mixture of acid and water. Different sounds made the diaphragm and wire vibrate at different speeds, which in turn made the wire dip into the acid-water mixture at different levels. This variation changed the amount of electricity flowing in the wire. A receiver turned this electric current back into sound again.

This was the first intelligible conversation ever held on a telephone.

In Bell's words:

'I then shouted into the mouthpiece the following sentence: "Mr. Watson – come here – I want you." To my delight he came and declared that he had heard and understood what I said.'

This diagram shows how Bell's early telephone worked.

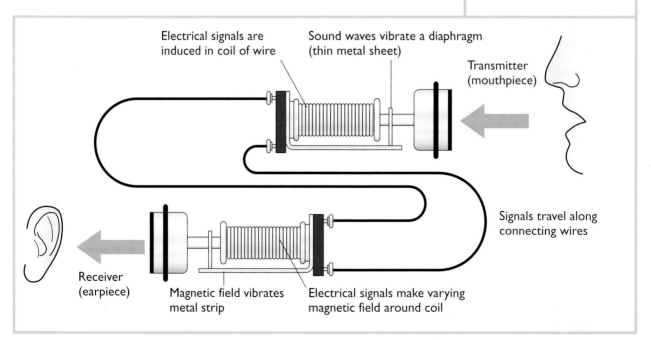

Electrical signals are induced in coil of wire

Sound waves vibrate a diaphragm (thin metal sheet)

Transmitter (mouthpiece)

Signals travel along connecting wires

Receiver (earpiece)

Magnetic field vibrates metal strip

Electrical signals make varying magnetic field around coil

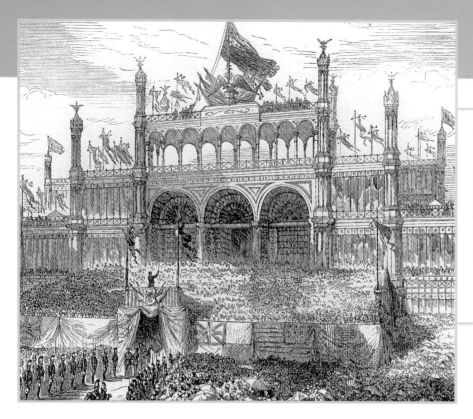

The opening of the 1876 American Centennial Exhibition in Philadelphia. Aleck's telephone was one of the exhibits.

The breakthrough had been made, but even now Gardiner Hubbard was not convinced. An even greater challenge, however, was trying to convince the public of the uses of the telephone. Aleck needed a large public display in order to attract the support and money required to launch a telephone network that would challenge the power of the telegraph companies.

The opportunity arose when the 1876 **Centennial Exhibition** opened in Philadelphia. Many scientists and inventors from all over the world were going to be there, just the sort of audience Aleck needed to show off his telephone. One important person visiting the exhibition was Pedro II, Emperor of Brazil. Aleck gave him a demonstration of the telephone and the event was such a success that it made the headlines in all the newspapers the next day. Interest was growing.

ELISHA GRAY

Elisha Gray (1835–1901) was born on a farm in Barnesville, Ohio. He became a boatbuilder, but also worked on improving the telegraph. In 1867 he patented a telegraphic relay switch. This won him the patronage of the powerful Western Union Telegraph Company.

He claimed to have conceived the principle of the telephone independently in November 1875. But he did not pursue his claim until the huge importance of Bell's invention became clear a few years later. Then the Western Union Company backed Gray's claim and contested Bell's patent for the next four years. Gray continued inventing in electrical communication and became very rich, but he was always jealous of Bell's fame.

A useful device

News of the 'miracle' invention was now spreading fast, helped by the many lectures and demonstrations given by Aleck across the country. The world's first outdoor telephone line was installed on 4 April 1877 between Charles Williams' electrical shop and his house 5 kilometres (3 miles) away. In May Aleck and Watson held a telephone conversation between Boston and New York. The first business use of the telephone began in May when a line was set up between the offices and home of a banker. The telephone was now on its way to dominating the world.

All change

On 9 July 1877 the Bell Telephone Company was set up, with Aleck, Thomas Watson, Gardiner and Mabel Hubbard and Thomas Sanders as the shareholders. Hubbard and Sanders looked after the important work of making and selling the new telephones. Two days later, on 11 July 1877, Aleck and Mabel were at last married, and Thomas Watson was their best man. Aleck was 30 years old and Mabel 19.

Engraving of a public demonstration of the telephone at Salem, near Boston.

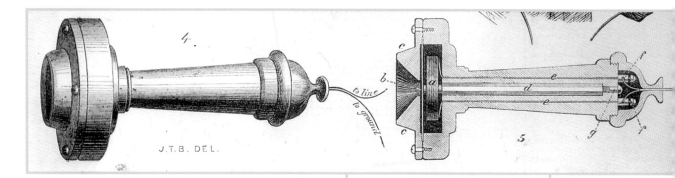

J.T.B. DEL.

The transmitter-receiver telephone that Aleck and Watson produced in 1877. This was the first telephone on which it was possible to hold a two-way conversation.

After a brief visit to his parents in Canada, Aleck and his new wife set sail from New York on 4 August 1877 bound for England. It was just seven years and three days since he had first set foot in North America, and in that time he had invented a device that was already beginning to change the world. Arriving in Plymouth, the couple travelled to London and Bath and up to Scotland to visit his childhood haunts in Edinburgh. In England Aleck gave a demonstration of the telephone to Queen Victoria, who later noted in her diary that it was 'most extraordinary'.

When Aleck eventually returned to Boston, he worked for a while with the Bell Telephone Company. But he had no head for and no interest in business. He once wrote: 'Financial dealings are distasteful to me and not at all in my line.' He was also growing tired of the telephone, and irritated and upset by lawsuits from other inventors who claimed to have thought of the telephone first. In 1880 he resigned from the Bell Telephone Company but he remained a shareholder.

In Bell's words:

'I went into his office that afternoon and found him talking to his wife by telephone. He seemed as delighted as could be.'

(Letter from Aleck to Mabel describing Charles Williams' telephone line)

Inventions and married life

Aleck was 33 and a very rich man. He could now devote his time to the thing that really interested him, inventing. This he did for the rest of his life. In the same year that he resigned from the Bell Telephone Company, Aleck was awarded the prestigious Volta Prize for science by the government of France. Aleck used the large amount of prize money (50,000 French francs) to set up the Volta Laboratory in Washington. There he worked on a device he called the 'photophone', which he regarded as his greatest invention. This used a vibrating beam of light to transmit sound. The Volta Laboratory also worked on improvements to Thomas Edison's phonograph (an early record-player).

Air and sea

Aleck worked on many other designs and inventions. He became especially interested in flying and designed many types of kite. One was a very light but strong design, known as a tetrahedral kite.

In 1908 Aleck and his design team built an aeroplane called *June Bug* which went on to win the Scientific American flying trophy. They designed other successful aeroplanes, including the *Silver Dart*. Aleck also designed a high-speed boat called a hydrofoil, which used skis to skim over the surface of the water.

Aleck in about 1903, holding a model of his tetrahedral kite.

The first successful hydrofoil had been built by Enrico Forlanini of Italy in 1900, but Aleck's work improved the design. His HD-4 hydrofoil was 18 metres long and was powered by two 350-horsepower engines. In 1919 it reached a top speed of 114 km per hour (70.86 mph), a world record it held for ten years.

Aleck became a respected leader in the world of science and invention, and the man who had never completed a university degree was now showered with honours from universities in North America and Europe. He revived the ailing *Science* magazine and helped to make it the success it is today. As a co-founder and president of the **National Geographic Society** he set this society on its way to becoming an international success.

Mabel and Aleck and their two daughters, Elsie and Marian.

Mabel Bell

Mabel Bell (1857–1923), Aleck's wife, was one of three daughters of the Boston lawyer and businessman Gardiner Greene Hubbard. She was born on 25 November 1857 and lost her hearing when she was 5 years old as a result of scarlet fever. She and Aleck married when she was 19, eleven years younger than him. They had two daughters – Elsie May, born on 8 May 1878, and Marian 'Daisy', born on 15 February 1880. Later they had two sons (Edward and Robert), but both died in infancy from breathing problems. Mabel had no more children and never got over the loss of the two boys. Elsie and Marian married and had a number of children of their own. Mabel gave $20,000 of her own money to set up the Aerial Experiment Association (AEA), the organization behind all of Aleck's flight experiments.

The final years

Aleck never forgot his work teaching deaf people to talk, and he continued to help people with hearing and speech difficulties. The money earned from some of his inventions went towards converting the Volta Laboratory into the Volta Bureau for the Promotion of the Teaching of Speech to the Deaf. He also continued his campaign to change the way people saw those who had hearing difficulties.

Passion for inventing

Turning his attention to medicine, Aleck designed a probe (a slender instrument) that could be used to find bullets hidden inside the human body. This made it possible for doctors to treat patients with gunshot wounds more successfully. It was used for many years, until replaced by X-ray photography. As a result of the deaths of his two infant sons from breathing problems, Aleck designed a vacuum jacket. This was a forerunner of the **'iron lung'** and, when fitted round the patient, used air pressure to help them to breathe.

In 1886, Aleck had bought some land on Cape Breton Island in Nova Scotia, Canada. Its wild beauty reminded him of his childhood holidays in Scotland. There, he and Mabel had a large holiday home built which they named Beinn Bhreagh, which means 'beautiful mountain' in the Gaelic language. For the next 40 years they spent every summer there with their daughters, and in time with their daughters' growing families. Aleck also built a laboratory next to the house so that he could continue with his experimental work even on holiday.

Aleck opening the New York to Chicago telephone line in 1892.

Beinn Breagh, the house on Cape Breton Island in Canada, where Aleck and Mabel spent every summer.

In Mabel Bell's words:

'This morning we drove to the New Glen, and saw forest-covered hills, undulating valleys with trim, well-kept fields and neat little houses, pretty streams ... I think we would be content to stay here many weeks just enjoying the lights and shades on all the hills and isles and lakes.'

(Mabel Bell's description of Cape Breton Island)

It was at Beinn Bhreagh that Alexander Graham Bell died on 2 August 1922, with his beloved Mabel by his side. He was 75 years old and had been busy inventing right to the end. The funeral was held two days later, and when his coffin was lowered into his grave near the house all the telephones throughout North America fell silent for one minute as a mark of respect to the father of the telephone. Mabel, brokenhearted, died five months later and was buried beside him at Beinn Breagh.

Bell's legacy

This mobile phone is also a video phone – the two people can see each other as well as speak to each other.

Alexander Graham Bell was a man with a burning curiosity about the world around him, and his passion for invention touched very many different areas. But his name today is forever linked to the telephone. The Bell Telephone Company grew into American Telephone and **Telegraph** (AT&T), which is now one of the richest companies in the world. AT&T established the Bell Laboratories where experiments could be made on the development of the telephone and other forms of communication. This is now one of the world's most important centres of scientific research.

A shrinking world

The basic telephone that is used today still works on the same principles devised by Aleck Bell. But there have been many changes and improvements in dialling and switching systems since then. Aleck had the idea of 'talking with light' rather than using electricity to transmit sounds, and most of the main telephone networks today use light. The sound signals consist of patterns of laser light beamed along filaments of flexible glass called **optical fibres**. These are thinner than a human hair and can carry thousands of phone calls down a single strand. **Digital** transmission now produces better sound and cheaper calls.

The radio was invented by Guglielmo Marconi 26 years after the telephone. The two technologies have been combined to create a communications revolution.

Instead of wires, telephones can now use radio waves to beam signals from one side of the world to the other via satellites far out in space. This has led to the dramatic increase, since the early 1990s, in the use of small, hand-held mobile phones which can be used practically anywhere.

Other kinds of information, apart from sound signals, can now be converted into electrical or light signals and sent down a telephone line. In this way, letters, illustrations and information stored on computers can be passed to facsimile (fax) machines from one side of the world to the other in a matter of seconds. Without the telephone, the Internet – which relies on phone connections – would have been impossible.

Legacy to the deaf

Aleck's methods for teaching the deaf are still practised in schools throughout the world. The Alexander Graham Bell Association for the Deaf, based in Washington, DC, is now the largest organization for the education of deaf people.

The telephone has taken over our lives and transformed communications and human relationships in ways that would have been unimaginable in Aleck's time. Thanks to his brilliant imagination and inventiveness, and his belief in the importance of communication using the human voice, the world has become a smaller place.

Timeline

1847	Alexander Bell born in Edinburgh, Scotland. The first commercial telegraph line in Edinburgh is opened.
1851	The first underwater telegraph cable is laid under the English Channel between Dover, England and Cap Gris Nez, France.
1855	James Clerk Maxwell devises a mathematical equation to explain the transmission of electromagnetic forces.
1858	Aleck goes to the Royal Edinburgh High School. He adopts the name Graham and becomes Alexander Graham Bell. The first transatlantic cable is laid between Ireland and Newfoundland. Charles Wheatstone patents an automatic telegraph system.
1861	A telegraph line is opened between New York and San Francisco.
1862	Aleck leaves school and stays with his grandfather in London for a year.
1863	Begins teaching in Elgin, Scotland.
1865	Father produces the Visible Speech alphabet.
1867	Brother Edward (Ted) dies.
1870	Brother Melville (Melly) dies. Aleck sails to Canada with his parents.
1871	Begins teaching deaf children in Boston, Massachusetts, USA.
1872	Starts experiments on the multiple telegraph.
1873	Appointed Professor of Vocal Physiology at Boston University.
1874	Makes his first sketch designs for a telephone. Gardiner Hubbard and Thomas Sanders become his financial backers. Thomas Watson becomes his assistant.
1875	Aleck patents the 'autograph telegraph'. Accidental discovery with the plucked reed. Engaged to Mabel Hubbard.
1876	Patents the telephone (Patent no. 174,465) Sends the first telephone message. Demonstrates telephone at the Centenary Exhibition, Philadelphia.
1877	Marries Mabel Hubbard. Bell Telephone Company is founded. Thomas Edison produces the musical phonograph.
1878	Daughter Elsie born in London. Joseph Swan invents the electric light bulb.
1880	Aleck resigns from the Bell Telephone Company. Second daughter, Marian, born. Awarded the Volta Prize for science.

1881	Aleck and others invent a wax cylinder for Edison's phonograph. Emile Berliner patents a gramophone using flat discs. Son Edward born and dies.
1883	Son Robert born and dies.
1885	Heinrich Hertz demonstrates the existence of electromagnetic waves.
1886	Aleck builds a holiday home on Cape Breton Island, Canada. Heinrich Hertz begins research that demonstrates the existence of radio waves.
1888	Nikola Tesla invents the induction electric motor.
1895	Wilhelm Röntgen discovers X-rays.
1898	Valdemar Poulson designs the forerunner of the modern tape recorder.
1902	Guglielmo Marconi transmits the first radio message across the English Channel.
1908	Aleck and colleagues win prize for the first manned flight of more than 1 km (0.6 mile).
1911	Marie Curie receives the Nobel Prize for her work on radiation.
1915	Aleck opens the first transcontinental telephone line between New York and San Francisco.
1919	Aleck's hydrofoil boat breaks water-speed record.
1922	Alexander Graham Bell dies at Beinn Breagh, Cape Breton Island, Canada, aged 75.

Places to visit and further reading

Places to visit

The Science Museum, London, England

Explore Bristol, Bristol, England

Manchester Museum of Science and Industry, Manchester, England

Millennium Point, Birmingham, England

Alexander Graham Bell National Historic Park, Baddeck, Nova Scotia, Canada

Alexander Graham Bell Homestead, 94 Tutela Heights Road, Brantford, Ontario, Canada

The National Museum of American History, Washington, DC, USA

US Army Communications-Electronics Museum, Fort Monmouth, New Jersey, USA

Websites

British Telecom's Innovation and Technology Showcase: www.bt.com/innovation/index.htm

Treasures of the Science Museum: www.nmsi.ac.uk/on-line/treasure/index.html

The Telephone History Website: www.cybercomm.net/~chuck/phones.html

Futher reading

Langley, Andrew and Williams, Brenda: *Victorian Britain* – History of Britain series (Heinemann Library, Oxford, 1994)

Oxlade, Chris: *Light and Sound* – Science Topics series (Heinemann Library, Oxford, 1999)

Parker, Steve: *Telecommunications* – Twentieth Century Inventions series (Wayland Publishers, Hove, 1996)

Shuter, Jane: *Communications* – A Century of Change series (Heinemann Library, Oxford, 1999)

Glossary

acoustics the science and study of sound and the sense of hearing

anatomy structure of the body

Centennial Exhibition an exhibition held to celebrate the 100th anniversary of the independence of the United States

deaf-mute person who is deaf and cannot speak

diaphragm thin, flexible screen or mesh

digital transmits information such as sound as a series of digits rather than as waves

electromagnet type of magnet produced by passing an electric current through a coil surrounding a soft metal core

electromagnetism the magnetic forces produced by electricity

elocution the art of speaking clearly and distinctly

Industrial Revolution a period of history when working practices and conditions were changed dramatically by the introduction of mechanization

iron lung rigid case fitted over a patient's body, in order to help him/her to breathe

lawsuit proceeding in a law court brought by one party against another

magnetic field region of magnetic force surrounding a magnet or an electrical source

magnetism the power of attracting or repelling iron

National Geographic Society a scientific and educational society established in 1888 in Washington, DC

natural philosophy physics

optical fibres thin glass fibres through which light can be sent

parchment type of paper sometimes made out of animal skin

patent government grant to an inventor giving him/her the sole right to make, use and sell the invention for a set period

phonetics sounds made by the human voice, and the study of these sounds

physiology the way that the body works

Smithsonian Institution an institution based in Washington, DC that provides funds for research and runs museums

telegraph a system for transmitting messages across distances using electricity

Index